NAFSI
Jihad upon my Self

POEMS *by*

Kashmir Maryam

ISBN-13: 978-0692679364

All praise is due to God.
To my parents, whose love and sacrifice have
taught me that wisdom stands on the loyal legs of patience.
To my husband, who has entrusted me with his heart.
To my siblings, Aishah, Naqeeb and Hamza,
who have shown me the thickness
of blood.

CONTENTS

ACKNOWLEDGMENTS

My dear parents, to whom I am forever indebted to – I cannot thank you enough; you have taught me the value of principle, in a world that favors assimilation and trends. You have taught me that strength comes through faith, and thereafter, in being steadfast. Indeed I have won the ovarian lottery- and my fortune is your love for me, and it shall be spent in my service to you.

To my intimate friends and my closest confidantes, who constantly enrich me with profound insight, and continued advice. Truly, it is sincere advice that is the manifestation of a refined and strong bond of sisterhood, and brotherhood.

To Khadijah and Paulette – my mentors. It was through you that I found my power with words. You nurtured me, and you believed in me, at times when I felt defeated. Thank you.

To my grandmother. It was towards the end of your life that I began to write this book, and it was soon after your death that I was propelled to complete it. I speak for you, in the language of our ancestors – in poetry. We may not have the ability to reclaim our land in Kashmir, but let me revive what I can through this tongue, which swells and flourishes with the herbs of the Himalayas. Let these words heal. More importantly, let them be a tribute to the legacy that you have inspired in every soul that occupied your presence. Both in life, and in death, you inspire.

May this book be a dedication to our lineage - that does not climb through Kashmiri valleys, but it climbs through the trees of Prophets, and eats from the fruits of a divine wisdom.

INTRODUCTION

There are some moments in life, when the soul is so close to the brink of reality, and then, it is dragged back to the illusion of this world by the iron hammer of its sin. Its fingernails dig into the earth, and its scratching can only be captured by the inscriptions of the pen.

We now live in an era where war has become beautified, and peace has been made cowardly. We live in a world where we have become so overcome by the deceptive belief that success comes through amassing the material, that rarely does the soul revert to introspect. Instead, opulence and all of the human temporal desires have been made false Lords to weak and enslaved souls.

Seldom is the sick soul recognized, treated, and permitted to heal; seldom is the soul consoled in its weeping – which manifests in the body's dissatisfaction with all that is worldly. It is for this reason, that you hold in your hands the calling to a spiritual revolution; I write to liberate you through reclaiming your authentic and truest Self. I must warn you, that there will be anarchy. There will be blood. You will hear the inward clanging of iron swords. You will feel the agony on the lips of each wound, speaking from within. But be assured, that after every storm, there will be Peace.

I have been summoned by a need to illuminate minds that have succumb to the rhetoric that the Muslim is strange- that the Muslim should be feared. I write with the sword that I am most familiar with- that is my pen. I write to declare *Jihad* on the thing most worthy of defeating, that is my soul – the *Nafs*. The *Nafs* linguistically refers to the agency of the soul, when it is in a state of being attached to the human body; it is responsible for exercising choice, or free-will.

Jihad is not to be misinterpreted as the murdering of innocent civilians. *Jihad* is not committing heinous crimes in the name of God. Rather, *Jihad* is the war that is waging within each and every one of us. It is toil. It is testing. It is sufferance. It is striving, and failing. Then learning and rising. It is the utility of the material for the serenity of the soul. It is war. It is submission. It is peace, and then emancipation.

We must defy our greatest enemy – our Selves. We must reclaim our seat in the kingdom from which our nefarious Other has dethroned us. Our limbs must be governed by principles, and we must empower our souls to be conscripted as our allies – not as our adversaries. We must restore the camaraderie of spirit and flesh. To be kind. To be loving. To be self less.

This is the premise upon which I write. I declare *Jihad* - upon **my Self**.

The heart is like a bird: love at its head,
and its two wings are hope and fear

- Ibn Al Qayyim

FEAR

War

I

War is waging.
Sword in mouth.
Mallet in mind.
The heavy word[1]
carefully balanced
at the tips of tongues.
It must equal
the same weight
as the heart,
Else this soldier
will lose his footing
and fall - before war
has even begun.

See-sawing between desire and devotion:
This battle will push man to his limits,
with every thing that he loves,
and no thing that he detests
As much as his mistakes.

The enemy will come forward
with a sweet aggression,
bearing the façade of love.
He will fight your tears of repentance -
Forcing them to remain in the ducts.
And reluctantly he will feel the pain of salt
on the lips of a believer.
A believer who understood
that in knowledge is power,
as he reflects on a revelation
which first commanded him to *Read.*

- *Conscripted*

The heavy word is 'laa ilaa ha illAllah'- the declaration of faith, which closely translates to "There is no true Lord worthy of worship, except Allah."

II

Fight.
Fall.
Rise.

Every day is a *Jihad*[2].
Tongue – cloaked in the dress of war.
Frail. And ready to be defeated.
It is this weakness
that binds me to being
a freedom fighter.

Ah, liberated by my limbs!
But what use is it if
I am chained from within?

What am I fighting for?
Why must I sacrifice that which I love-
for that which I need?
Spiritual being – are you seeking hope
through material means?

I, whose only qualification is conviction.
This spoken letter can only be closed with the final seal.[3]

Fight.
Fall.
Rise.

---

2. *Jihad* is an Arabic word, closely translated as 'struggle' or 'striving'. *Jihad* is commonly misconstrued to be a violent concept. In fact, the Prophet Muhammad (peace be upon him) referred to the greatest *Jihad* as being the one in which we struggle against our own selves. In this context, *Jihad* refers to the struggle against one's inner self.
3. Muslims believe that the Prophet Muhammad (peace be upon him) is the last and final messenger i.e the final seal of all the prophets; Muslims believe that there will be no true prophet or messenger to come after Muhammad (peace be upon him).

III

Oh clay creation,
So pristine is your face,
But how deep is the despair
housed within your soul!
Seeking a guidance,
But arms so tangled in the *dunya*[4].
Little time to raise them or prostrate.

Eyes distracted by the shape of her thighs
but how dishonest is he,
who will catch you
in the excitement of your desires.
Inciting you towards the
obedience to your Self.
And obeisance to a system
that takes joy and family life –
then recycles it to make macs and droids
to enter the circle of this commercial void
that lasts 74 years so when that Day comes-
all the wires that chained you to earthly living
could not hold your soul
from being ripped from your body.
And all that shall transfer
is your account of moral currency
made up of deeds done purely in His name.[5]

For now, swing between hope and fear.
And remember,
That you will never believe,
until you are ready to receive.

---

4. *Dunya,* in the Arabic language, is used to describe the earthly world, associated with the temporal and material nature of the transient life.
5. This refers to the name of *Ar-Rahmaan,* which is a name of God in Islam; it means 'The Most Merciful'.

IV

Who shall break the sword of my enemy?
That time has sharpened,
by the favors gifted upon whom He chose.

My Lord! Clothe me in silk
And house me in a heavenly abode,
So that my enemy
Shall never pervade
A realm into which he was forbade.

My Lord! Make blunt his dagger,
For my frontal vision cannot perceive
what lurks behind
And feeds, from the delicacy
of my molded spine.

- Child of Eden

V

Inhale - blood through your palms.
Grasp onto the knives that scar,
then strengthen.

Inspire - the musk of death in the air.
This is Carthage.
And you will fight,
with every piece of cartilage and soul,
To defend honor and home.

The residency is within,
and it is these internal wars,
that will leave the deepest wounds.

- Conscientious Consent

VI

Where are those who promised me respite
when the armies came with their tantalizing vows?
They promised me a life of splendor,
and forgot to mention an eternal doom.

Where are those that had the duty upon them?
To preserve my love for Him[6],
And to call me to the straight path.
To befriend without motive
Except that it was for Him.

- Comrade

---

[6] 'Him' in this context, refers to God.

VII

The prick of pain must be felt
In order for pleasure to be understood

- Purge

VIII

Sometimes you must watchfully retreat,
In order for your aggressor to blindly advance.

- Vision

IX

We are told,
that excellence speaks for itself.
What about struggle?

Does it speak?

Or is it made mute by men
who believed it should be men
who must write history.

- Herstory

X

Let the knife with which they pierce you,
become the pen with which you write.

Let the house of judgment that they build for you,
become a palace in which you sleep.

Let the thorn with which they prick you,
become the needle that stitches
the tapestry of your success.

Soul

I

Benching the weight of my soul.

II

When the cry for life screams ardently,
Seeking the ear most connected to its soul.
It finds that voice boxes like to bellow,
with few that hush upon the vision
of the lavish beauty, silence.

It ushers sound to the caves
of thought,
where in can ponder,
in its silent echo.

- War cry

III

The greatest lies are the ones
We tell ourselves.

The greatest sadness -
Caused by our own hands.

The greatest loss,
Is the one we inflict
on our own soul.

- Autoimmune

IV

Open your heart
As you would open your palms.
Receive love,
As if it is life.

V

The prayer that you drag your feet to,
The deceased would crawl to.

VI

We snorkel in the same coral reefs,
See different colors of the same spectrum,
    that mesh with forgotten dreams - never pursued.
We are champions,
Afraid to lose.
Lost deeply in the ocean of our own grieving shades of blue.
Wave upon wave,
    Seeking hidden treasures that our lower
    pirates buried.
But desire does not make a trustworthy map,
    As the compass of the soul
    becomes discordant
    when the voyage is struck by Wild winds.
Egos torn make excellent paper planes,
    as close as origami gets to unfolding fate.

In her body lies
    Folds and lines,
    For her to glide.
Whilst all her life she assumed her highs and lows
    were a consequence of those around her.
It was what lay buried inside her,
    that made her spirit stand and walk
    when her body was tired
    and ravaged by life's trials.
She is a consequence of her own actions
    Breathing. Because God gave her another breath,
    Believing. Because He opened her heart.

- Mermaid | divinely-aided.

Clay

I

Oceans displace genetic affiliation.
But the helix cannot be split-
only stretched across the pacific.

If the mind recalls,
then there is no need for phones.

It is as if the present can erase the footsteps you ingrained
in a similar-structured kind of clay - to you.

But for the time being, the reflection of my nose
in the mirror, shall be enough to remind me
of the power of familial relation -
that I will so proudly carry forth.

Even if it was flawed
I would find peace in its structure,
Solace, in knowing how close it resembles
The Oak Tree.

- Bint

II

A sinner bewildered in the burning Eden;
This jungle has Mowgli[1] lost after knowing the truth
but he has nothing but snakes in the wilderness to abide by
because humanity turned their back on a 'lost' cause
that was searching to be found.

Double standards blind our eyes,
Blindfolded twice - with sin and desire.
Conscience becomes divided,
Feeling sorrow at our progeny's demise,
Should not these deeds have become
filtered through the ages?

Intent is promising, commitment wavering.
In a storm most unsavory.
Faith broke with the chains of slavery.
Seeking out every disease of disbelief.

Iblees[2], so amused
at how his seed, in the human heart grew.
Only at death will it sprout
Tangled, untamed and impure.

Him free from blame.
You the accused.

---

[1] *Mowgli* is the protagonist of Rudyard Kipling's 'The Jungle Book'
[2] *Iblees* is what Muslims believe to be Satan's original name.

III

Strange.
You pivot along
the axis of destiny,
Victim of gravity.
Surrender to He.

Fail.
Fall.
Wake.

And revolute.

IV

Know your cause.
Stand resolute.
And do not fear
the consequence
of the consequence.

V

Petrified souls, inside vessels

that carry them

to a deed that

screams not to be

Committed.

It must shape itself

before a time

when an angel

shall pound a hammer

against a forgetful forehead

that never tasted the sweetness of

P r o s t r a t i o n

VI

Life on this Earth is but a day.

All the vessels on its shelf

will eventually

s h a t t e r

VII

It is not the strength of our enemy that shall defeat us,

It is the weakness buried within our Self.

- Cemetery of insecurity

VIII

Oh forgetful slave!
You tasted freedom
before your stomach yearned for it.
You testified to a message
before your soul and body were joined.

Oh forgetful vessel!
You are spirit in clay,
And you think that to display
the clay is more liberating
than to unclothe the soul?

Oh naked slave!
Why do you speed towards your doom
On a path where thorns
can scorn your exposed skin?

- Insaan | Nisyaan

IX

And to what displeasure do I owe
the account to sway towards
a truth that does not sow
an ounce of action?

Even if it were for a pound of flesh,
this miserly body
knew how to take from others
and to give, in sin, to its Self.

- Nafs Al-lawwaama | The Reproachful Self

X

Why do you settle with dust
when you were flung into the air?
Your trial should have defied gravity.
It should have made feathers of your burdens,
and shaded you with light.
So that you would rise against the odds
like the raindrop, that falls on a hot summers day:
The moment it hits the earth, it rises again.

- Phoenix

XI

What injustice is there greater
than the soul that screams for peace,
Whilst the voice of man roars with laughter
so violently destructive
it ripped its clay to shreds
of empty stone – impermeable.

If only, it could learn how to repent.

- Blood from a stone

XII

When sincerity becomes scarce,
and arrogance becomes abundant.
When a lie buys trust
and then trust evaporates
with the lives of the trustworthy.
When worthiness is sought through validation,
So that a menace can claim a pretty prize
just because she did not know her value.

- ConFounded

XIII

Their tongue utters something,
but their eyes - they tell a different tale.
It seeks fulfillment in its vices,
because it forgot the Verses[3].

---

[3] Verses here refers to the verses of the Quran.

XIV

You believed,
so you were tried.
You desired,
so you were of those whose
appetites swayed with the
movement of the pendulum.
Moving on every axis,
and defeating all logic,
Because desire is in the mind,
and the mind is all in your mind.

- Swoon

XV

This soil I tread on- it speaks.
It tells me to listen carefully
as my steps are numbered.
It tells me to seek nothing more
than which is promised onto me.

The corruption within myself cannot do harm
if it is contained and chained within this vessel.
Oh my Lord! Keep it chained.
And let it not possess any control over these limbs.

I am the child of Adam - predisposed to flaw.
Let fear and hope bring me to you in one piece-
not ravaged by the canines of my disobedience,
but with the softness of my molar teeth.
These molar teeth that clench onto the rope
that you Revealed to me.

Prepare me for Goliath, and armor me
with the ability to distinguish
between the whisperings, and your call.
For your call cannot be mistaken,
but my ears can be deceived.

- Litany

XVI

Obedience calls to the humbled gaze
lowered by the windows of the soul.

Man is the most quarrelsome of opponents
but the devil has him on his knees
Reeling for the next moment his lusts
dictate his next fix.

He claims to be from dust but he is mixed with fire,
and kindles destruction that could nullify his every seed.
Genes that mutated from prophetic trees.

That sacred lineage diverted by honey
that did not come from the bees.
It came deceitfully just like the forbidden tree,
and it told you to drink.
To quench yourself, but the thirst is real,
when you make your Lord second
to the crack the devil deals.

- Fiend

XVII

Know where you stand in the struggle.
Made from the same clay,
our hearts separated by an ocean.
We divided like continental shift,
tectonic plates raised us -
the mountains echoed 23 verses
of your chromosomes
which aligned straight enough
to formulate a poetic existence.
Stitched together,
I am the tapestry of your effort,
the evidence of your struggle.
The witness of your pain.
My smile and my frown are
synchronized to your state.
The Simba of your pride.
The mix of seven tribes.
I speak a language from five others derived.
A product of colonialism,
I am English and inclined
towards Shakespearean vibes
And William Blake's rhymes
that commercial lyricists of today's industry deny.
Those that make consumerism divine,
Materialism cannot make one spiritually high.

XVIII

How can the practice of wrong,
make you rightfully rise?
I shake every palm tree
that hides in Zionist lands
because if roots were legs,
you would see them walking
across the border - into Palestine.
If very leaf was an arm,
you would see trees
holding the deceased;
Weeping willow for
children whose dreams
still sit on their pillows.
As bombs fell into their cradles,
you would see leaves covering their honor
as nature hates that which is not natural –
It delays its witness of our abuse on its soil.

I declare faith:
Laa ilaaha illallah
And if this is ever forgotten,
it would be because we forgot ourselves.

- Canaan

XIX

Travelling on the same rocky boat
that led to assassinations and a police state.
I feel the potent prick of the same needle
that inflicted metro-viruses into educated minds.

Be the voice that tells the people
that freedom is not found in books-
It is found in hearts.

Tell them,
that seeking the truth comes
with educating the youth.

This is the name that both writes
and fights for rights.
This is the hand that destiny took
from slavery to insight.
This is the hand that fights
for holiness amongst the divide of a holy land.

XX

How can we thrive when we walk back
to the caves that our ancestors crawled from?
Animalistic, with instincts only on preserving
the human race, for the sake of the race.
In the process - lose face.

Gain temporary pleasure in a fleeting world.
In the lying face, honest eyes reside.
Souls torn between pity, and hate.

- Ne-man-derthal

XXI

It is sink or swim,
Or is it in synch with sin?
Either swim deep with sharks
Or glide shallow with dolphins.
I am sinking, but I am swimming-
I am butterfly-stroking my way
to the light
that shimmers between
the waves of darkness,
that pull me,
then push me
using aqua physics to play
with my metaphysics,
But my soul- it does not jest.

Am I a mermaid,
so Aerial, but not sufficient because
I fail to be fully Aryan?
Life flips me choices like the split in my tail;
The pearls that sit in my veil
will tell that tale
to the one who is strong enough to lift it.
Persistent enough to prize it.
Willing enough to resist it.
No fighting, only writing,
Spoken
Mouth to mouth,
Heart to heart.

It is either sink or swim,
Am I in synch with sin?
Or do I trust my trust in Him.
It is time to close my eyes,
and fall back into the waters
that dust and soul
separate me from.
It is time to lose my breath,
if it means gain in intellect.

Waiting for the tide to rise,
so that I can fly to the high skies
on the tips of hardship,
reclining on a bed of needles,
Washed to shore.
But my thirst calls me
back to the waters,
Unable to live without it,
Wishing to be without it.

- Glide

XXII

Eyes silvery, like moon-reflections
as her visual field splits into walks of life.
Old age makes a fool of a fool
but makes wise of the praising.
Memories map timelines on her wrinkles.
As she smiles, her paths seem less jagged,
As the corners of her mouth
make round any sharp region.
She is a century old daughter
of a Queen, of a Queen, of a Queen.
They say she breathes her last breath,
but her shaking hand
clasps with strength.
Mother of a nation.

She inspires my body, mind and soul.
Her touch make the spaces
between my fingers whole.
She is the golden ticket
wrapped in golden skin.
Not an ocean can divide us,
Nor can any Hater's hate, or Envier's envy
divide these seas of devotion.

- Grieved and found relief | Your grandchild

Woman

I

Covered for so long
he forgot the shape
of her legs.
But like pegs,
they are mountains.
They stand resolute
when the earth quakes.
But turn to dust
when the verses echo
in the lagoons of her uterus.
She is whole, yet hollow.
Incomplete, except when
she conceives the
thoughts of her Lord.

- Conception

II

You provoke,
  but do not feel.
You control,
  because you fear.
You distance,
  because vision becomes unclear.
You tighten,
  because your whip, it does not fear
To fall on skin
  that does not tear.
You collapse,
  on what does not shatter.
What is broken,
  when emotions are invisible?
But it is battered
  by abuse which does not flatter
The ego which seeks dominion
  of a Queen, whose rule is over
  her inner Kingdom.
 Whose dignity remains,
  even when treason knocks
  at the palace gates
Dressed in the cape of an ally.

- Treason

III

A diamond shall never
reduce in its radiance
in the sight of other rubies.
Its shine comes from within.
Its polish comes from
the repentance of sin.
It shall never be destroyed
by jealous claws that gnaw
at human weakness,
In order to glorify
what insignificance signifies.

- Thy neighbor

IV

Be far removed from the leaves of ivy -
they enjoy the beauty of the darling roses,
so long as they do not flourish
in their territory.

- Emerald City

Earth

I

Can the purified spirit
Love anything that is impure?
Can it build clock towers that
tower over a people who have
lost time to the promise
of a deceitful liar?

We live in the dimension
of love for this life
and the promise of a hereafter.
But the barrier between,
is a restrictive seat
in the grave of the one
who would not submit,
To the Lord of all worlds.

- Renegade

II

When I traverse the earth –
The scorpion adorned like a bride –
Am I numb to its poison?
Or do I walk broken-backed,
unknowingly carrying its burden?
This world of plastic and
alluring decoration.
This world that we spend
Our lives buying everything for,
But it would sell us in the blink of an eye.

- Prostitute

III

How transient is this earth,
that tilts upon its axis
wayward thinkers
who believe that the struggle
of soil made from soil,
is all in vain.

- Delirium

IV

Hate weakens,
what love betroths.

Envy burns,
what faith constructs.

Arrogance deducts,
what mercy puts.

V

Do not love too excessively,
Nor hate excessively.
Else you will hurt excessively,
And lose excessively.

- The golden ratio

VI

This morning I woke up to life.

Its splendor.
Its disaster.
Its richness.
Its poverty.

I woke up to hidden truths,
And apparent deceit.

But the earth – it moved on its axis,
Serenading me,
with each phase of the moon.
It rocked me back to my slumber.

- Lulla-Lie

VII

How forgetful we are,
  losing sight of our blessings
  when pondering over affliction.
When the world is turned upside down,
  it is because we made it an oxymoron,
  and it is indeed fixed back to its original state:

The wealthy,
  who become more withholding,
The poor,
  who would give anything.
The friend
  who becomes the enemy,
The enemy
  who seeks friendship.
The lovers,
  who only hate,
The haters,
  who only love.

- Paradox

VIII

How can I see it any other way
when I am standing at the source
of where light is diffracted?

I witness possibility in five different states
    as the light breaks into a spectrum of situations.
Observing the pomp and glitter
    of the life of the world.
Ripping at the seams with hopeful promises,
    and false nothings.
Walks of life,
    chosen by the boots that bear
    the strength of your soul.
Whether they carry water
    or carry holes.
Pretty soon you will see the paint crack
    with smiles,
And the oak walls will show beneath their age.
It is then that you will realize the distance
    between Adam and his progeny,
Is just as an apple,
    that does not fall far from the tree.

- Congenital

IX

In the midst of Babylon calling:
Paralyzed souls laying bricks on high buildings,

 built on the cemeteries of our ancestor's ships.

We worship sky scraping tips
 then complain our necks crick as we look up.
But in truth, it is whiplash

 as we fell so hard from the heavens -

 all our souls remember is a blur of images.
But how well do we put the pieces together?

The jigsaw will not solve itself
 until we realize that we do not need to try

 so hard to fit in – we are already placed.

Hands so dust filled and mauled by the earth.

Feel the soil's skin as it generates and regenerates

 against coarse palms just awoken.
The universe a level playing ground.

Dust of unknown consistency,
 waiting for its judgment.

We have the identity of one print.
Instead, we photo-copy
 and have become a product of factory lines.
Born into tribes
 but dividing ourselves with knives.
Everything we like, we subscribe to-
 but this is not Netflix,
 this is every episode of your life.

When the issue having four wives consumes the media
 more than a man cheating four times.

At the same time, we are told that less is more

    so that we start wearing less, thinking it is more.
But then skin care companies tell us to cover
    to prevent melanoma -

So confused and used by this commercial world

    we do not know how to think for ourselves.

It has tapped into our subconscious as it caresses human greed
    because let us face it – we have become so plastic
    we cannot bleed.
The construction of Kindle Fires

    so that we can artificially read.
We are still slaves,
    raising wrists chained to our own chest -

    proclaiming that we are freed.
Creating test-tube designer babies,
    now we even artificially breed.

In the midst of Babylon calling:
Paralyzed souls laying bricks on high buildings,

    built on the cemeteries of our ancestors ships,

We worship sky scraping tips
    then complain our necks crick as we look up,
But in truth, it is whiplash
    as we fell so hard from the heavens –

    all our souls remember is a blur of images.

But how well do we put the pieces together?

- Neo-Babylon

X

Sacrifice is what we bleed.
It is in the book that we read.
The thought that we conceive.
The eradication of the evil seed.

Sacrifice was the action of *Ibraheem*[1],
and every other prophet
because of the strength of their belief.

It is the pedestal upon which faith is conceived.
It is the circus that distinguishes
the tricks of *Shaytaan*[2]
and the afflictions on the soul.

It is pleasure through pain.
It is the loss that must be felt, before the gain.
It is the prick of cold that touches
the camel's skin in Antarctic terrain.

Sacrifice is not about losing the values
that tucked you into bed at night.
It is holding onto them.

- Endure and elevate

---

[1] *Ibraheem* is the Arabic name for the prophet Abraham, who is also recognized in Judeo-Christian scripture.
[2] *Shaytaan* in Arabic refers to an entity that is devious and rebellious. In this context, *Shaytaan* refers to Satan.

XI

Hearts tumbling
from failure to understand.
Desires rumbling
when what is right
trespasses into what is left.
Wrongs are justified
by right intentions.
But action does not
synchronize with virtue.

You saw it.
You desired it.
You pursued it.

So you drank its lies,
deceiving both the body
and the conscious mind.

XII

We often say things that we do not mean,
And mean things that we cannot speak.

XIII

Oh haughty eye!
That is offended
when its vision is not caressed.
Oh ego! Flee from the caves of the heart,
And touch not the inner crevices
of my primitive art.

Oh Traveller!
Who voyages towards
the mirage of delights.
Hold onto the coal of your faith,
And let it burn through your
skeletal, calcified desires.

- Hubris

XIV

Oh eye of mine!
Did you see the dazzling sight
of bright smiles and weak hearts?
Did you open your shutters
to let a thousand arrows in?
Did you permit the poison
of their envy caress,
then sting your optic nerves?

Oh eye of mine!
You are only as humble as the mind
that guides your visual impulses.
Direct your sight to mountains, that sit like pegs.
And rivers, that praise your Lord
as they flow towards their destination.

Oh eye of mine,
Close yourself
To see what the world
will not show you.

XV

And doesn't life
lose all its splendor,
when one realizes that
the proximity of death
is between two fingers.

XVI

When the bringer of Death
arrives without invitation.
When man smells his deeds
and sees the world
that he was veiled from.
This is when he will be reminded,
that he shall be held accountable
for all ills that his wicked hands pursued.
.

- Die the way that you lived

XVII

Run away from the world,
Watch how it chases you.

Tongue

I

The point is not the point.
It is the blunt edge
that delivers the mark
as wet ink feels no belonging.

It bleeds into the scrolls of papyrus,
joint lines in matriarchal monarchy.
When paper clasps pen,
and then the two
cling to inspiration.

The point is not the point.
It is the tip that stabs
every joy and hope
that destiny must fulfill.

The point is not the point
of fountain pens with two split ends
that ink shall swim divided through.
falsehood will perish,
and the truth will remain.

The point has become
the point of no return
As the *fat-ha*[1] has elongated,
and the *kas-ra*[1] has impregnated
to produce the most beautiful words[2]
that you will ever hear.

The point is not the point,
It is the soft edge
that moisturizes the tongue
with its compassionate syllables.
It caresses the mouth and the heart
In the brutality of turmoil.
Revealed to the orphaned[3]
and revealed to the mothered.
A truth most beautiful,
both when veiled,
and uncovered.

---

[1] *Fat-ha* and *kas-ra* are both vowels in the Arabic language.
[2] The 'beautiful words' refers to the revelation, i.e. the words of God revealed unto the Prophet Muhammad (peace be upon him).
[3] This is a reference to the Prophet Muhammad (peace be upon him) who was orphaned at a very early age; both of his parents had passed away in his childhood, and he was then placed under the care of his grandfather Abdul Mutallib.

II

I have heard articulate liars.
I have seen sick-minded healthy people.
I have felt the prick of nationalistic pride.
I have seen those from aristocratic heritage
behave more savage than
the layman without privilege.

I know of those beautiful wives
who are adulteresses.
I have seen people from the street
with deeper insight than doctors.

Success is not this. It is not waking up
and counting the worldly assets you possess.
It is waking up and being happy to have nothing.

III

The purity of the tongue
is groomed by the
steadiness of the heart.
When it wavers,
the tongue slithers
somewhere between toil
and betrayal.

IV

Tongue held in paralysis.
Numbed, whilst this heart
feels the pain of loss.
But the mind reminds
of the gain.

V

Soul,
Converse with me.
Why do a mother and father
fight so silently,
so selflessly?

- Fruit of the womb

VI

Think
About every thought
that surpassed
the gauze
that tastes
and lays
behind the sabered tooth beast
that beats
the believer
with his tongue.

Master of rhetoric:
one who masters nothing except
further inquiry into the question
of the question
of the question.

Let me introduce to you -
Magicians of articulate speech,
to words that are greater
than what mountains can bear -
The speech of your Lord.

So I speak,
To the one who forgets
that this religion is complete:

*Ilyawma akmaltu lakum deenakum
wa atmamtu alaykum ni'mati wa
radeetu lakumul islaama deena*[4]

Faith will free you-
both aristocracy and slave.

---

[4] This verse is taken from the Quran (Chapter 5: Verse 3). The *Muhsin Khan*
translation of this verse is as follows: 'This day, I have perfected your religion for you,
completed My Favor upon you, and have chosen for you Islam as your religion.'

VII

Beware of a time
when your garments may cover you,
But your tongue unclothes you.

- Shameless speech

VIII

When envy displaces love
between brethren,
and judgment precedes
the seventieth excuse[5],
Then surely the speech we
deemed most trivial[6],
shall be made up of whips
that will cut out a pound of flesh
which could have loved stronger
than the tongue
that hated.

- 'If you prick us, do we not bleed?'

---

[5] It is reported that Hamdun Al-Qassar, one of the early Muslims said: "If a friend among your friends errs, make seventy excuses for him. If your hearts are unable to do this, then know that the shortcoming is in your own selves."
[6] This is a reference to frivolous speech such as gossip and backbiting.

Appetite

I

When mercy disappears,
there shall be nothing left
Except empty stomachs,
and salivating mouths.

When love dissipates,
the thread between the animal
and man, shall snap
And the saber-tooth and the claw
will come together
and shall tear to shreds
What the bricks of patience
and the cement of tears,
from the weeping
of a reliant slave,
took years to build.

II

Revelation falling on the heart of man,
but the unexposed soul seems to grasp it better.
So now the eastern essence in western eyes
lies somewhere between mystique and fear.

What is this belief that bedazzles the hearts,
yet controls the deed?
Fed by the hunger of the fasting stomach.
Felt by the power of a prostrating back.

III

Estranged from worldly ornaments,
She becomes familiar with her soul.
Restraining outward glances,
the light entered the windows of her soul
and it did not want to return
back to the earth.

- Deflection

IV

Rebellious soul
in the act of sin.
You tasted lust
and drunk in
intoxication.
Your sins
must rest in the seat
of the fasting limbs.
Occasionally you
shall hear them breath
with a fire that will never be as hot
as the coal[1] of my faith
that resides in my palms.
Tied around all fingers,
Shining bright
like a star amongst
Black holes.

---

[1] Abu Hurayrah, a companion of the Prophet Muhammad (peace be upon him) narrated that the Prophet (peace be upon him) said: "A time will come upon the people when the one who is patient (in them) in his religion (will be) like the one holding onto hot coal." [Collected by Tirmidhi]. This narration indicates that there will come a time when society will be afflicted by many trials (i.e wickedness, lewdness etc.), and the believer will find it very difficult to preserve their faith. Holding onto one's faith under these conditions is compared to holding onto hot coal in the palm of one's hand - implying that this will be a challenging and trying time.

V

When hunger shakes,
and thirst distills
the sin upon which this
human acted.
Shakespearean words
cannot prepare
the believer
for a greater tragedy
Than letting this month depart[2]
having received only
hunger and thirst.

---

[2] This is referring to the month of Ramadhan, in which Muslims, during daylight hours specifically, must abstain from food, drink, backbiting, lying, and sexual relations, to name a few. Some individuals are excused from the obligation of fasting, such as young children, elderly people, the sick and women who are pregnant.

VI

In the pursuit of happiness
did we forget our souls?
Too busy satisfying eyes
and stomachs.
We are residents
swimming in luxury,
and despair,
In the belly of the whale.

VII

You will find in the cave of solitude,
a paradise for the hermit.
And in the crowds of full stomachs
and starving hearts,
A hell, disguised as a paradise.

VIII

What is the rope of Allah?
The rope that nurtures the human
In the belly of the earth;
The umbilical chord that could
just as easily tangle the throat
of the gluttonous child -
forty years young,
who speaks in seven tongues
in different tones
dependent upon the listening ear.
That eats through seven stomachs
and grazes upon its brother's flesh.
Why then abstain from food and drink?
Whilst you fill your stomach
with the meat on your brother's bones?
Often envy is the evil root
Of this forbidden fruit.

Rabb

(Lord)

I

Face to hand.
Palm to sky.
Tongue to praise.
Praise to Allah.
Eyes to prostrate.
Sujood[1] to *khushoo*[2].
Love to sacrifice.
Sacrifice to patience.

---

[1] *Sujood* is an Arabic word, which translates to 'prostration', i.e. the physical act of placing the head on the floor in submission.
[2] *Khushoo* is an Arabic word, which translates to mean humility, tranquility and devotion in prayer.

II

Worship flies,
just as wings separate, then rise.
Faith sat firm in the feathers,
and love to guide as it glides,
through tides and treasures.

Winds of the soul's pleasures.
Appetites never fully conquered
as the bird of life stands like a phoenix,
and travels through the secret
dimension that the mind harbors.

No ill thoughts, as faith cured the unthinkable.
So instead the soul diverts
its thoughts to the One who created it.

III

Can you taste faith?
Can you taste that which innately
grows at the back of your mouth
and at the tip of your tongue?
Can you taste what suckled you
from *fitrah*[3] and in *fitnah*[4].
That which your soul tries to savor,
and your foes try to destroy within you.
They cannot touch what was divinely put.
They cannot shake the foundations
of what was built in His name.

---

[3] *Fitrah* is an Arabic word, which does not have an exact English equivalent. However, it has been described to closely mean 'primordial human nature', which is an innate disposition to believe in one God. The *fitrah* is believed to be the state in which mankind is born into - a state of purity, and a state of clear and true understanding.
[4] *Fitnah* is an Arabic word, which has extensive number of meanings, depending on the context in which it is mentioned. In this context, *fitnah* refers to 'temptation', or to 'a trial/ tribulation'.

IV

Runaway.
I am running away
from desire and consequence.
Escapism in defeat,
or is it escapism into victory?

Unleashing of true authority,
which is no authority
except that which is divine.

Reliant on the earth's compass,
I look for another world.
Travelling on a prayer mat,
I see the same sides of a different spectrum.

The *Imaam*[5] carries me with his voice.
I am a wayfarer seeking the road home.
Looking for the quickest way
because I carry a heavy load.
Optimists vision through a shattered lens.
I see cracks that make up
the kaleidoscope of my soul.

---

[5] *Imaam* is the Arabic word, which in this context, refers to the individual who recites the Quran in the congregational prayers in the mosque.

V

Welcome to the war of reason versus roses.
The onslaught of a dialectic tongue
Unable to explain to the spear of the heart,
why it must let down its weapon
in order for the peace
to put at ease the limbs;

The two could once understand one another.
Now, ignorance and submission to desire
dictate the ammunition of the tongue,
with the zeal of a crusader,
who will not stop after four thirds
of the belly have drunk blood.

This alabaster soul, delivers a fury
that cannot be silenced until
recollection and remorse
clean away the dark spots
that cancerously mutate.

It aches.

It asks.

Do you not know that the greatest beauty
emerges from the greatest ugliness?
To change is human nature,
we move from state to state.
From love to hate.
From glory to disgrace.
From face to face.

- Duplicity

VI

Praise of His name.
No human hand
can tame, weaken, or defame.
He rearranged hemispheres of the earth,
and cortexes of the brain -
Programmed to praise his name.
No one fails except him who
did not study the universe
close enough to see the signs.

In nature, in nurture,
in cultivation and in culture.
This world is a metaphor of the rapture.
All souls in the bodies captures
prisoners for a while.
The sinner's cry echoing on the clay walls
that the human anatomy contrives.

Now I remember why I forgot.
See, I travelled in my dreams
where my soul witnessed my body
in a distant land,
where time was not measured by sand
but by the metaphysical mind.
Made God-consciousness derive
from my subconscious.
Made to verbalize experience
in words that rhyme,
Reading around at His signs that surround me,
I read aloud messages mimed to me -
because nature does not lie.

It cries.

HOPE

Shield

I

Drink the ink of pens

and spill the words that armies fought

in the name of.

Let each bead of black and blue

be the weapon with which you slew

each ill-wisher, cloaked in the wool of sheep.

Who would dance upon your grave,

Just as they danced around you –

as actors, within a play.

II

Live humbly
Die honorably.

III

Greatness can only achieved through sufferance.

IV

Justice speaks louder than voices.

V

What can they strip from the
cloak of your honor,
Except that your skin
will reveal the map of the lands
that you fled to
in the midst of the war
that they declared upon you.

- Atlas

Cavalry

I

Did you know that the whale
has the loudest sound known to man?
But the silence of self-reflection
Greater.

It penetrates dimensions
That the soul has yet to know -
That the body tries to make sense of.
That the genetic code shall never reveal.

It is hidden, and it is yearning.
For the body to reclaim its soul.

II

And isn't every soul,
when distanced from bodily need,
deemed introvert?

Nothing matters except internal mirrors
built around the mirror
of the believer's pupil.

Reflection is more than a scientific concept
Of lines and points.
It is enchanting and defining.

It is filthy earth pondering up a perfect Creator.
Seeking to be cleansed.
Seeking to be found.

- Voyage

III

Who shall heal
this wounded soul?
That must love
in order to find,
what patience measures
in heavenly reward.

IV

The word
Flows from the mind,
rolling across synapses.

Departure from the tongue,
Final terminal -
the heart of another.

Relator of inner secrets
Body language speaking for you.
Revealing in full swing,
with eyes that smile and sing
the happiness of the soul.

- Conductional | Conditional

V

What is more profitable,
than that which money
cannot feed?

Nor does it eat from the
trees of greed.

It calls to the calming of the soul.
Caresses the body
in its time of need.

- Solace

VI

When beauty subsides,
what is left, except decorated pottery,
and a cracked soul?

VII

Shape.
Pots made from a clot that was shaped
and left to formulate
into the thinking specimen of a human.

Intellect.
When the soul was blown
and Behold, life was given.

The thinking mind,
so mindful of the second blowing[1].
Knowing it would be risen
by the yeast of its fermented
struggle.

- Rise

---

[2] Muslims believe that the Day of Judgment will commence after the angel called Israfeel has blown into the horn (trumpet). Scholars of the Quran believe that the horn will be blown into twice; they derive this from the verse in the Quran (Chapter 39, Verse 68): **"And the Trumpet will be blown, and all who are in the heavens and all who are on the earth will swoon away, except him whom Allah wills. Then it will be blown a second time, and behold they will be standing, looking on (waiting)"**

Nafsi

(The Self)

I

Wild heart,
Be still.
And anticipate
the jungle of peace.
Which in the thick of the night,
burns through the limbs
with a piercing light.

Be still.

And apprehend
the melodious call[1] as
it elevates you when
you recite as much
as your heart allows you to.

Wild heart.
Be still.
The Mowgli from within,
may have been raised by wolves
but his status is above angels.

---

[1] This refers to the recitation of the Quran, which Muslims believe is the word of God, calling one to the truth.

II

Silence beckons even the loudest of spirits.

III

If you want to know a man,
Place him in a room of beggars,
And see if he shall treat them as kings.

IV

When the night envelops
all that unknowing eyes presumed.

When the night absorbs forbidden speech
and cuts valleys through the rocks of hearts
that thrown upon the table
maintain poker faces.

But honored are the queens of all suits
who conquered their souls,
and sought victory
in the last third of
every night[2].

---

[2] The 'last third' of the night is regarded as a very extraordinary time for Muslims. This is based on the statement of the Prophet Muhammad (peace be upon him), who said: "**Our Lord descends to the heaven on the last third of every night (in a manner that befits his majesty), and He says: "Who is calling upon Me that I may answer him? Who is asking from Me that I may give him? Who is seeking My forgiveness that I may forgive him?"**

V

When destiny
paves a rocky path,
embrace all stones.
And build within
the storm,
a home.

VI

Chasing dreams like eagles.
Sometimes the dream is beneath us.
We must hover in order to discover it.

When the claw seizes it,
we find, that imagination
venerated what was a pauper
dressed in Royal clothing.

So now return to reality,
that snatches without courtesy
the dream that can only exist
within the imagination of the eyes.

VII

A beggar with faith
is greater than a king without.

VIII

Blind yourself to what good
your hands put forth.
For it is the truly virtuous
that do not consider themselves so.

IX

Sit with those who possess
the wealth of knowledge,
even if they have not even
a penny to their name.
And leave those who persist
in the poverty of ignorance,
even if they owned the clothes
on your back.

X

Didn't you know that grown men are
supposed to cry.

That pretty girls are most prone
to being insecure.

That it is the last leaves of fall that
Look most beautiful.

That there are full moons
to fill empty hearts.

XI

It is compassion that makes men.
And strength that makes women.

XII

You may see my victories,
but you do not see the losses
that made me work for them.

XIII

Sometimes it is the cracked heart
that knows best how to heal.

XIV

Dig,
even if your hands refuse

Sow,
even if your seed is weak

Reap,
even if your soul is tired

Love,
even if your heart has stopped.

XV

Sometimes you must lose in order to find.
You must bruise in order to heal.
You must cry in order to see.
You must smile in order to live.
You must die in order to survive.

Toil

I

Engage people with your silence,
for it speaks mountains.
And know, that mountains
do not speak – they echo.

II

The fact that it is forbidden,
should be more overwhelming than
the fact that it is beautiful.

III

There was a day,
when you exceeded in your efforts
to please the one who
was blind to your value.

But just as the sun must rise,
So too, must this white cloud.
Now it moves to another land,
And here, the rain grows fields of flowers.
Each face – shining just as bright as its neighbor.

IV

With every pattering drop,
I see a new hue in the rainbow.
It screams color,
and it silences rage.

V

Very few friends requires she,
whose pen and paper meet at dusk.
Writing in gold ink,
in the company of the moon.

Treaty

I

I waited,
one hundred sunsets for a day
when the sky again
embraced its guest[1].
Whose beauty is cloaked
in mercy and musk,
so when the stars declare
their praises for Allah tonight,
I shall grasp onto thirty days
of spiritual appetite,
in this stomach that awaited
the entrance of our visitor;
Deserving the reception of a King.
For it is this month,
That shall rule our desires.

---

[1] This 'guest' is referring to the holy month of Ramadhan.

II

Will my worship be sufficient
to make one month enough
to redeem a lifetime of sin?

III

When the hours passed
like waves of renewal.
And the parched throat
allowed nothing to caress it -
except the blood of its prior sins.

When the tongue was starved
of all falsified speech,
And the soul was made replete
with forehead to the ground.
So dropped pearls and beads
from the devout mouth
that spoke nothing but beautiful vowels
Glorifying the words of Our Creator.

IV

Can you taste those words?
That depart with ease,
But are the hardest to swallow.

Those words that flourish like lilies
upon a moist tongue.
Listen to the flowers of speech
that are none other than what was
Revealed through *Jibraeel*²,
That came to us in a cave,
where The Seal of Prophets³ was told,
*"Read"*³

---

² *Jibraeel* is the Arabic name for the English Gabriel.
³ The 'seal of prophets' is a title given to the Prophet Muhammad (peace be upon him), who Muslims believe to be the last and final Messenger of God.
³ The first words that were revealed to the Prophet Muhammad (peace be upon him), as stated in the Quran, were: **"Read! In the name of your Lord, Who has created (all that exists)"** (Chapter 96, Verse 1)

163

V

Oh illustrious moon!
Whose presence marks
my beloved.
Whose reflection enchants
and beautifies.
Oh illuminating moon!
Your distance is enough to keep
away from the Earth's corruption,
but close enough to serenade
the insomniac's sleep.

Oh dazzling Moon!
Whose beauty was compared
to my Rasool[4],
Who was commanded
to split you in two[5].
Let me take a piece
and you keep a piece,
so that I can be reminded
of the beauty to which he,
Peace be upon him,
was greater.

---

[4] *Rasool* is the Arabic word for 'Messenger'; here 'Messenger' is referring to the Prophet Muhammad (peace be upon him).
[5] One of the miracles that the Prophet Muhammad (peace be upon him) was given, was that he was able to split the moon in two, by the permission of God.

VI

Will I ever taste the honey
of my people's faith?
The sweat that perspired off
living flesh that
Died 1400 years ago?
The family that I belong to:
My mothers who spoke poetry
to my Prophet.
Who articulated love through vowels,
and alphabetical curves.
When women of my era
strip their clothes
to attain that former glory.
But the body is only a vessel,
and speech- it is the musk,
That pours from this clay cup.

My people,
Did we forget the honor that faith gave?
The kind that Rome could not withhold,
Nor that the Mayan could have foretold.
It is an honor that is estranged
from extravagance;
it feeds mouths that denied luxury.
They did not devour the flesh
off their brother's backs[6].

The honey that they procured
Sits on shelves of stories past.
If only we could delve into the lives of the dead
Who knew life better than the living.
So sweet is the sweat that they exuded,
Running off their striped backs
because hardship is what gave them
that gold substance in their bellies.
These are the humble bees,
Whose honey from time to time,
Falls from the lips of scholars.

---

[6] This refers to individuals who did not backbite others. This is based on what is stated in the Quran, when God says: **"O you who believe! Avoid much suspicions, indeed some suspicions are sins. And spy not, neither backbite one another. Would one of you like to eat the flesh of his dead brother? You would hate it (so hate backbiting). And fear Allah. Verily, Allah is the One who accepts repentance, Most Merciful." (Chapter 49, Verse 12)**

VII

His back
Lined with the seal[6].
Can you feel his struggle?
It bleeds through holy walls
Broken and made whole
by the stones of Ta'if[7].
Can you hear his sandals,
That walked through
heat-clenched sands
In defense and in prayer,
For the nation he knew
would follow him. -
His beloved,
though he did not see us.

Do you see his footsteps?
They bear the mark of prophecy.
Can you see his path?
It is the one that is most straight, but it bears thorns
For the righteous road is the one less travelled.

---

[6] This refers to the Prophet Muhammad (peace be upon him) who was also known as the 'final seal'. The 'Seal of Prophethood' was also a physically seen characteristic that was prophesized in previous scriptures (the Bible and the Torah) that Muslims also believe in. It was an area of raised skin the size of a "pigeon's egg", between his shoulders; it was a region characterized by moles.

[7] Ta'if is a city that lies South East of the holy city of Makkah, in Saudi Arabia; it holds historical and Islamic significance due to events that transpired during the earlier years in which the Prophet Muhammad (peace be upon him) was given Prophethood. When the Prophet (peace be upon him) visited Ta'if, he spoke to the tribe of Saqeef about Islam and the oneness of God, he was received with great hostility and was stoned out of the city.

His body drenched in blood, the Prophet (peace be upon him) said: "I saw a cloud hovering above me, and lo and behold, I saw Jibreel (Angel Gabriel) come down from that cloud, and besides him was an angel that I had never seen before." And Jibreel said to the Prophet Muhammad (peace be upon him), 'Oh Muhammad (peace be upon him), your Lord has seen how your people have responded to you, your Lord has seen what they have said to you, so he has sent me with the angel of the mountains to place at your disposal.'

The angel said, "O Muhammad (peace be upon him), if you want, command me and I will cause the two mountains of Ta'if to collapse upon them. He responded: "No! Rather, I pray that Allah blesses their children to be Muslims and worship Allah alone. Even if they have rejected Islam, I pray that Allah blesses their progeny to be Muslim."

Love

I

Every kind of love bears its conditions.

But the smallest conditions,

the greatest forgiveness,

and the most affectionate love,

is from the One in whose hand

holds my soul.

My Lord, Most Merciful.

II

If the love for your sister

or brother

Disintegrated

because of green eyes

and black hearts.

Cleanse your spirit,

so that you both become

red like blood

and white with purity.

III

Wading in her waters,
I am seventy percent her flow
and thirty percent her dust.
I taste salt that dissolves
then resolves all determination.

Find me in the oceans of perspiration,
I will be speaking to the waves.
They can understand this language.
I must face the danger of their power
in order for me to find security.

I must remember the one who Created,
the One who will never forsake.
A pure love, that will never
humiliate or betray.

Let it cleanse,
Let it teach you its motion
That rises and falls,
just like the tides of belief
that sway with
the moon.

IV

The engagement with your Lord in the thick of the night
is rich and permeating. To undervalue the intimacy of private
worship for the enjoyment of public worship is like a traveller
who sees a well and an ocean. He attends to the well because
of the formality of acquiring water, but he misses the ocean,
whose vastness can only be acquired through solitude.

V

Is not love derived from sacrifice?
So that the sleeping lover
would give away his slumber
in order to be
with his beloved.

Is not love a consequence of mercy?
So that the mother's hearts
yearns greater for her Creator
than the child that sits
in her raised arms.
Is not love the twin of justice?
So that the oppressed
find relief in knowing
their Lord is The Most Just.

Is not love truest when filtered?
So that the parched tongue
finds hydration in the recitation
of a book where one letter
is worth ten deeds.

Is not love pure?
So that the filthy souls
find cleansing in the battle
with sin in tin hearts,
fighting me, with me,
with the steel of zeal.

VI

Love does not make jealous.
It protects.

Its delicacies are found through
earnest eyes.

It does not wane.
It strengthens.

Love does not ridicule.
It gives honor.

Love does not decapitate.
It unites.

Love does not capitalize.
It socializes.

It does not individualize.
It revolutionizes.

VII

Where are those
that love
one another.
For no reason,
other than that
they were
commanded to?

VIII

Frail hands,
you are most powerful
when tied with supplication.

Weak index,
you flourish when the contents
of your life direct your invocation.

Rabid claw,
you will only be as infectious
as your submission.

Webbed finger,
you shall wade through wisdom that
ancestral oceans laid.

Because your existence
is nothing except what He molded with
His own hands.

IX

Did I achieve success?
Did I sacrifice desire
in exchange for a reward
that is only with God?

Did my tongue submit to the paralyzed
position at the base of my mouth,
or was it acrobatically flipping
off the shortcomings of a believer?

Did I attain what my soul needs
or did I bleed without feeling?
Empty and distracted in kneeling.

Our Lord,
Accept the good that we
in earnest do.
As flawed as we are,
we try.

- Laborer

X

How irresistible is His calling.
When the ears have heard the verses -
how can music seduce one from the truth?
This melody - without instrument,
is the human voice,
that houses the sorrows of its soul,
it penetrates the soil of this withering rose,
and brings awakening to a dead existence.

Taken by the hand.
Rising with the sun,
and setting with the dust.
These sorrows sit with stars
as I carry my heart to
Witness His Dominion.

How is anything that I have
worthy to be given?

Offerings from a dependent soul,
Your hands already possess me.

- The Irresistible

XI

House of Allah.
Let Your walls speak to me.
House of Allah,
Let our souls reside in a
heavenly province.
Forever in your debt,
we seek for the platform
that will raise us so our tongue
can find its way
through the Arabic alphabet
to bring together
the praise of Your name.

Allah hu Akbar[1]

Let Your words echo
from the walls of Your house
through to the ears of my soul,
then to reverberate into my hands -
raising them to You.
Praise is for You.
Dominion is for you.
I am for you.
Forever in your debt.

Let the windows of your soul shut,
Let the eyes of the heart open.
I wake. A fumbling of colors swirling
like a beautiful tornado
in the forecourt of the house of Allah.
Tiles warm from the suns heat,
His mercy encompassing,
and the needle of my human pulse
directs my gaze to the sky.

I am a slave.
Desperately
in need of
my Creator.

- Darussalam

[1] *Allah hu Akbar* is an Islamic phrase also referred to as *Takbir*, meaning 'God is Greater'.

XII

Who said that that
which satisfies eyes,
can satisfy hearts?

Verily, it is the unseen
that consoles best
a weeping heart.

XIII

Come to Him broken.
Only He can make you whole.

XIV

Beauty can be found
through ink that runs
through the forests of paper,
so strong, it blots layers.

That same ink that runs down the
Valleys of her cheek
as pain mixed with kohl
clinging onto the hope
That He is her best friend.
He, who created her.

- Khalil

XV

With the submission of every limb
Comes the prostration of the soul.

XVI

What does it mean

To love?
To live?
To dream?

Nothing.

If you do not believe.

ABOUT THE AUTHOR

Kashmir Maryam is an internationally acclaimed writer and performer; she is a 3rd generation British-Kashmiri Muslim, born and raised in the city of Leeds (UK), now residing in the US.

Kashmir is featured in the movie 'We Are Poets', which captures her journey all the way from the red brick inner-city streets of England, to performing in front of the White House at 'Brave New Voices' – the world's most prestigious poetry slam competition.

Since then, Kashmir continues to deliver inspiring speeches, as well as performing her poetry on national and international stages. Through her spoken word, she encourages the need for self-empowerment through spiritual cognizance and unity, in order to ignite global change.

Kashmir is the Co-founder of The Strangers – a non-profit organization which is devoted to clearing up misconceptions about Islam, through the art of spoken word poetry.

More information on Kashmir's performances and appearances can be found on: www.kashmirmaryam.com

Regular announcements are also made on her social media accounts (Twitter/ YouTube/ Facebook/ Instagram) @KashmirMaryam

www.ingramcontent.com/pod-product-compliance
Lightning Source LLC
Chambersburg PA
CBHW030829090426
42737CB00009B/937